NOTEBOOK

RULED PAPER

THIS BOOK BELONGS TO:

____

authored by: Marcel Doll, Hammerschbüchel 10, 53797 Lohmar, Germany

Made in the USA
Monee, IL
14 January 2022

88969970R00069